Night Fable

Seth Jani

FUTURECYCLE PRESS
www.futurecycle.org

*Cover artwork, "Inner Life of the Mind" by agsandrew;
author photo by Taryn Hendrix; cover and interior book design
by Diane Kistner; Georgia text and Foglihten titling*

Library of Congress Control Number: 2018937285

Published by FutureCycle Press
Athens, Georgia, USA

ISBN 978-1-942371-51-9

For My Parents,
Who gave me a home in a place
Where I could still see the stars

Contents

Explorers

To critique reason,
I want to find
The one small door
The heart believes in.

The aperture between worlds.

I want to enter it as one would
A cavern after dark:

Small light, gentle fear,
A sense of deep beginnings.

Falling Asleep

Just before sleep
Strangeness fills my thoughts
Like a bite of nocturnal fruit.

It's been summer all day
But suddenly I can't recognize
The trees in their motility.

Like a butterfly hugging the bark
Of a dark cedar as the sun
Goes down,

I cling to what is still
Oddly familiar.
In the half-light

Even the shape of what
I love loses precision.
Every night we get to practice

This terminal art
Of leaving our bodies
And becoming someone new.

Moonstruck

The body like cedar dust.
The soul mastering oneironautics,
Passing through the slim door
Reflected in the water,
Or disentangling from the flesh
To alight on the small flowers
Of the other world.
Our lives are simultaneous
With that one,
And we dance in the two-footed darkness
Straddling the forgetful banks
Of sleep and small thinking.
To remember, to remember,
The one mantra we must recall.
To name again the logic-shattering death
That rips us, roots upwards, from the earth
Like love or mouldering,
Like the bright reflection
That drew Li Po
Into the moonstruck sky
Beneath the Yangtze River.

In the Rotary Silence of Seasons

There was so much worthy of attention.
The slightest angles of sun
In the crux of evening
Causing the leaves to shine,
Or filling the city with such exquisite light
That even the rooftops
Shimmered into flame.
There were the birds meandering home,
Needing no other comfort than the wind
Letting their songs float down like blessings.
But even among the unarguable splendor,
The ceaseless call to wonder,
The fullness of that loss grew fuller.
Like sand collapsing around the roots
Of a ripped-out cedar,
It swallowed the volcanic colors.
Not able to cope or wrestle
With such enigmas,
You turned your back on what was given,
Unable even to bear that bright, empurpled sky.

Two Worlds

Cumulus. Two mares spliffing the night
With their warm nostrils.

The moon like someone's large inheritance
Lost outside the window.

Ebb of darkness. Bleared horizon.
Death's small cassia in the neglected plot.

Roundabout in the gentle dreamscape
The oneironaut tumbles through the flowers

Searching for a sign. The mother of someone
He's not sure exists follows him until he wakes.

In the morning he finds birds
Composing near his bedstand.

While he slept their sound entered his dreams
As a mountain's distant singing,

A waterfall's voice, a lovesick phantom,
The small thump of a cardinal's heart

Which in the strange dark of almost waking
Whistled through his head like a peacetime air raid,

Like a massive stroke of light.

Horse Valley Nocturne

Clouds black as someone's passing out.
Birds like skeleton keys
Unlocking the sky.
Bulb-lit pages buzzing with texts
And codas.
Whiffing the luminous,
I trail my heartache
Down to the river's
Glass dominion.
I catch fish in the stone's
Small pools,
Watch dragonflies
Skirt like blue storms
Over the rifts and hedges.
I want no more stories
That do not lift me deeper
Towards the earth,
No more angels unless
They're black and full of worms.
The fireflies are like living sparks
In the mind of matter.
I catch one thought in my hand
And follow another
To some haunted oak wood.
There, they string the leaves
Like tiny ranges
Gas-ovening the night.
Death is like this,
The barely noticed breath
Of the other world
Permeating your lungs
While you sleep.

In your dreams it appears
As perfect summer clouds
Drifting over,
As someone's lost mare
Nudging your face,
Delicate and cream-white,
Her soft fur all you cling to.

Seasoning the Ship of Death

It drifts with no other cargo
But the salt of your experience.
The riches, pains, crystallized days
All sprinkled on the darkened planks,
The deep materials.
It has no name, no destination,
No captain but a strong, courteous wind.
And each grain, lost or added,
Causes beautiful delays.

Horses

The oneironaut unhinges a door
In his brain's strangest precincts.
An emission of blue light
Catapults through his mind
And he awakes with the face of God
Etched into his eyelids.
No one will believe there
Are waterfalls from another world
That submerge his heart in sleep,
That there are birds
With stained-glass plumes
Singing in his pupils.
The horses of his quietest secrets
Roam the darkened field
And not only do they really exist
But he leads them, night after night,
To stables of honey and gold.

Declension Music

The dreamer wakes up
Near the axis of the dream.
The trees there are blue,
The ground made of fire,
A cold fire, and the other world
Where he sleeps is only
A splinter of memory
Fixated between the moon
And a thin, vitreous cloud.
In this place, the heart proves
To be made of plurals,
Papier-mâché birds who roost
In the shape of a body.
He can feel his awareness
Grow scattered, each twittering thought
Pushed towards the boundaries of the dawn,
Its white fractals.
Whatever names signify
In our austere cognition,
They are only music now—
Reels of deteriorating polyester
Looping back, again and again,
In the dreamer's mind.

NIGHT FABLE

Nothing's changed, other than the night
Cool as someone's desperation,
As the land of absolutes
Transmogrifying shapes,
Breaking open like
A ruptured skull.
Where the village recedes
On the shadowed hill
A mare walks enamored.
Each step causes blossoms
To spiral from the earth,
Puncturing the sky with constellations.
To be here is to witness the way
The night creates enigmas.
Where something solid, defined
By sunlight, stood in opposition,
There is now only the milk-white mare
Fading into dark. It is said that someone
Once followed her, and that the memory
Of that moment became the source
Of all goodbyes.

Night Birds

His cartographies end
Just at the edge of waking.
He can map the amorphous shapes,
Liquefied shorelines, pint-sized houses
Of his sleep, but when morning nudges
At his hand his compass breaks
Into bits of disassembled light.
He fears citizenship among
The solid dynamos, the world
Of manufactured forms.
Every evening he waits for the calando
Of night-singing birds over the horizon.
They pass through him like a superstition.
He never recovers from his sense of awe.

BROKEN HULLS

Do you require anything
Of the ocean?
It's been gathering our
Darker factions
And is now a world of secrets.
We can love it the way
We love dried flowers
Pressed between pages.
Their beauty astounds us,
Though we will never know
Their full circumference,
The fields where they bloomed
Centuries ago,
Or the hand that tore them
From their dominion
To preserve their final, fading blues.
Wherever those ships
Were headed, the eels light them up
Like storm-filled windows.
The shape of all we know
Is defined by that beautiful,
Fragmented flash.

Borders

There is a gate in the body
Where confusion escapes like
A bird, like anger stoked into
Wisps of smoke.
After the long channel of sinews,
The rivers of blood,
It enters a clarity,
A pinpricked luminescence
Too small for clear logic,
For solid forms of thought.
Only confusion, muddled
Like nocturnal trees or
Bleared palettes of blue,
Can key itself into shape.
Not every country can be mapped
By waking delineations.
Some borders only stretch
The haunted road of sleep.

The Glassmaker

Every moment we are sinking
Into the labyrinth of burnished light.
Into the place where the leaves
Are like contrails,
Like smudged dragons of smoke.
If this is the same place
That sleep takes us
With its weighted necklace,
Perhaps it is also
The upper echelon of death,
The blue apartment where
Consciousness flicks its moth-like
Wings into silence, into shuddering nights.
On the other side will we even remember
The textures of fear and longing?
Will we recall how we wished
For crystal bodies impervious to wind?
What is solid in us
Is also just a veil,
Thin as the delicate stamen
In the glassmaker's imitation rose.

Conduit

It blew straight through the dreamer's head
The way a star crashes to earth
And water fills the gorge reflecting back
Its absence.
His dreams filtered out and populated
The world with marvelous altercations.
In his sleep, a simple light kept burning.
A white poltergeist, torrential snow,
A perfect chord struck and held in resonance.
After images comes a beautiful silence,
The hole in the sky which the mirroring river
Turns into a second emptiness.

STARLIGHT

Black gaze of starlight
Keeps entering the farmhouse
To overturn the establishments
Of milk and honey,
To hover near the pilot
Admiring such fierceness.
And like a ghost of the open prairie,
Or the spin of dark nebulas,
It snows down, pockmarking
The kitchen floor,
Challenging the sleepwalker
To find his way.

Knowable Bodies

The oneironaut doesn't fear death
Because the landscapes dissolved in sleep
Are also the landscapes in the brain's
Erasable murals.
He doesn't identify with them,
Neither the grass blades in the meadow,
Nor the white animals lumbering through
The stalks like gods.
He is closer to the moon, zenith-height,
Observing everything. Although even that
Is saying too much. The moon is part
Of the fabricated valley and even in the crux
Of such beautiful objects we must refuse
The radiance.
The oneironaut is unwavering in his lucidity.
He keeps his gaze fixed on something
Far beyond the orbit of knowable bodies.

False Maps

Sometimes the birds are misconceptions
In the realm of trees.
They flare into untruths, and people
Follow them like false maps over the horizon.
They lead into blues that are really
Rooms inside the dreamer's head.
We sit inside them, absorbing color,
Becoming something other than ourselves.
It's a long way between the arc of transparency
And the opaque world in which we live.
Only birds can get there—or maybe the
Logic-cutting wind, blowing its austerities
Across the roof.

Botany

Dreams are a geography,
Another world neither here
Nor in the brain's receptors.
We are alternate inhabitants,
Natives of many layers.
The birds, too,
Who know all the wind's dimensions:
Night squall, summer's breath of fire,
The star-encrusted glyphs
Of winter air.
A thousand different dialects
Spoken and maintained.
When we love this world
In all its iterations,
We start to hear
A compendium of vaster things.
Far from waking,
There are flowers that only bloom
For the drunk and heavy sleepers.

What's Gathered There

It's there in the dark
Like someone's plastic saint,
Like a child's model train.
Around it the wicker ends
Of the light keep burning,
Keep pushing back
Against the great black spiders,
The emissaries of night.
It's shaped like one or two
Gnarled elms on the witch's hill,
Like a molted dream
In the dim and greening silence.
It's hidden in the planks
Like a corpse or termite,
Like a trapped, speechless wind.
From it we learn the language
Of walls—
Why they always creak,
Or drip in soft water.

Populating the Dark

Kami, like light or pollen,
Renegade music at the forest's edge,
Are always showing
In the bleared treetops
In the cosmonaut's dreams.
They are ruptures in the casual routine,
Sleights in the daily business,
Sudden flowering gods
Secretly upsetting the office order,
Or more intently
Driving the market crash,
All those well-dressed jumpers
Tumbling overhead.
Sometimes I catch them
In a lightbulb,
Strange filaments of smoke
In the curving glass,
Late-night whispers
That startle me from sleep
Like splitting tree limbs
Or a deceased relative's
Half-remembered voice
Drifting in from the cellar door.

Teeth/Canary

Marigolds, little sun askance
On Newton,
Other roads heading west,
Somewhere a passage east,
A door in the canary's skull
Where we learn some kind of yoga,
A balancing act between worlds.
Or better yet, a portal in the dark
Leaves of summer,
A temporary mouth
Through which we pass,
Quietly dazzled.
No one knows where
Besides the wind,
Besides the small mouse
In the fairy tale's semicolon.
The heart has this way
With things.
It transforms,
Magicfies.
We are so pinned up
In our logic
We forget it was the
Heart's invention:
Old codex tried on
In the long, mysterious grass.
Unneeded now, I'll take
The blue-notched stars
With their flaming centers,
The dissolving bones
In the sea's arched chalice,
The little whispering friend
Who can cross the dangerous threshold
Thin as a cricket's tooth.

THE ALCHEMIST

The alchemist is turning himself
Into a bird laden with flight.

It's Wednesday and the caravans
Of shoppers pass through
The procedural darkness, their faces
Soft stones whetting the light.

He watches from his window,
Drawing mandalas from the dust
Of a midday windstorm which settles
On the sill like somebody's ashes.

For all the gold he cannot make,
There is still the transmutation
Of longing, the sand traps of desire
Edging their way to music.

His magic is as complex
As any game of the mind's devising.
Beyond economics, beyond
The shadow-boxing of being,

He is filling the world
With a nameless water, an elixir,
A liquidity of dreams, washing off
The heavy slough of reason.

He is reminding us that we are
Tiny mirrors, lovely lights catching
Flame at the edge of every season.
He is the soul's last tinkering mechanic

Undertaking the great work of changes
In his library with no doors.

ZODIAC

Nobody can glean a meaning from the house.
Its angular shadows stand
Like black lions in the corners,
Like a resident darkness that
Stretches on for centuries.
Rooms that take up entire floors
Are no bigger than a closet,
And cupboards have dimensions
The size of small countries.
You can ride a horse across
The black fields of the hall,
Or drown in the oceanic tub.
Likewise, lying in the master bed
Is no different than being cauterized
Across your body.
The blankets smell of cinders,
And when you awake, your dreams
Fill the room with smoke.
There are no alarms other than
The clang of ancient rusted bells
Hidden in the walls like bodies.
The doors in and out are zodiacal.
They follow the stars
On their crystal circuits.
Mastering astronomy is how you escape.

THE SLEEPWALKER

He was always a morbid convalescent
Who couldn't tell dreams
From the economies of daylight.
He was always recovering
From this or that fantasy,
Charting diagrams of made-up cities,
Mixing colors in hopes of remembering
Shades he invented in his sleep.
Sometimes he believed somnambulance
Would lead him to invisible doorways,
Though he always returned soaked
In rivers, nearly frostbit by the winter moon.
Whenever he wrote, his poems were
Indecipherable, slim trees crooning
Against the darkness, language extracted
From the night bird's nest.
One night he even found an egg
Bright as raw pearls. He lifted it
From the tree and consumed it whole.
He floated everywhere.
It turns out it was a balloon
Drifting in from someone else's
Celebration.

Waking Up

It's where the border breaks
Into a mirage of daffodils.

Where the water shines
Like stretched metal.

Where a blue finch's whims
Leads you on a summer's day.

It emerges from the fog-addled eye
Of the deep circumference,

A jolt in the brain's machinery,
A passing through.

From the dark, collective waters,
The memory-voiding sea,

It gradually appears:
Green motes, neural tinge of light,

The beautiful vehicle of the body's motion.
We move through the familiar space,

Piecing together the painted fragments—
Trees, cities, your brother's rusted car—

The entire wavering kiln suddenly full
Of such hard and dreaming clay.

Into Matter

The soul translates
To a mustard-colored bird,
A stygian heirloom
On darkened banks.
It is a seed
Or maybe a star
From other,
Radiant hungers.
When it comes down
It's like a paulownia leaf
In lateral sunshine.
We hold it up
To shade our bodies,
Or cup great mouthfuls
Of rain.

CALANDO

When the bird falls into sleep,
His dream is the color of old medallions,
Axinite meadows where evening throws
Its fables over the grass.
Seeing that place in a small glint
Between trees,
I listen closely for the way
The worlds touch.
Wherever the bird originates from,
Its song belongs equally to both.
We don't know what is real.

What Gives Us Weight

As always, more of us falls
Sidelong with the rain.
Molecules steeped
In the yellow mud,
The delicate cores of frost.
This flesh, we say,
Is primed for condensation,
For the tinkering beads
Of ocean foam,
For the water the moon
Lifts in its quiet vessels.
Whatever separates us
Is a thin glass of frozen air.
The liquid quarts
Inside our bodies
Are waiting to burst.
When they explode,
Those blood-soaked rivers
Will form a sea.

An Exchange of Wonder

When the images begin to falter,
When they slow like metastasized light
Dripping from the maples,
The soul unhinges from the body
And plank-dives into the colonies
Of roots,
The loam and fractals of the other world.
Some days you might hear it,
Someone's last flicker
Transitioning off the phone lines
Down through the static wind
To haunt your door,
Or lingering in your inner ear
Like a secret ocean.
Golden pop and sizzle,
Covenant of mythic birds,
The continual chatter backroom
In your brain
That we call reactive
Though we know there is
A constant exchange of wonder
Burning in the bloodlines,
A miracle of cells and ashes:
The whole world
Meticulously rebuilt
Before our sluggish eyes
Can even acknowledge
A fire has occurred.

ALL THIS SINGING

This bird floating downriver with only its head
Buoyed above the waters
Recalls Orpheus in the flow of his final singing,
The way even trees seemed to bend
Into a blooming reception,
Or how wild animals gathered from the fringes of the wood
And understood that this was music.
Sometimes I feel the need to forget the city
And vanish into some small green refuge
Or drink a friend's concoction of powders and pills,
Wanting even in delusion to catch a shining vocal
From some god in passing.
I find little comfort in our sterility or reason.
So much electricity is burning in the world,
The real kind, white and absolving,
Like that found in the pulse of oceans,
Or in the terror of a night alone, far off
Inside a mountain.
At times in the rare wavering before sleep
Even my own house dissolves, in its place
There is a cascade of submerged voices
Like that from this floating bird, and I am shocked
Into something wonderfully unnerving,
A bolero of flame and moonlight,
A nakedness before the fog.

Ghost

The migrant shadows
That are the leaves
At the end of autumn
Passing now into other
Distant summers,
Rust-colored worlds
Far from here,
Are like small birds
Debating the dust.
Alternately feathered flame
And vanished body,
Eternal substance
In the spectral drift.
And when we lie under
Their flickering enigmatic light,
We too are half root and sinew,
Half verdurous ghost.

Being Here

These days among the flowers,
Among the swirling light
Of avenues and yards,
Among the calm acceptance
Of the oaks and poplars,
Are perfect luminous intervals
Lighting the marginal darkness
Of a life.
Like Hell, we say to the great weights
Of circumstance,
Like Hell to the physics of failure
And loss.
Summer days filled up
With something romantically simple:
Longing and absolution,
Loving the inescapable,
Clouds forming shadows
On the neighbor's lawn.

SUMMER TREES

Nothing here, either awake
Or in the infinitudes of sleep,
Will prepare you for the shimmering
Hand scooping your body
From the earth.
No thunderclap, no raven's caw,
No beautiful meditation
On stilled objects.
Even in the ruins of our logic,
We travel towards the mystery,
Freighted and opaque.
To be translucent doesn't take
Understanding or quantified expertise.
It takes a heart porous as summer trees,
Each piece of exploding identity
Passing through as if it were
An outer element:
A particle of migrant pollen,
Or the diamond-cutting rain.

REMAINDERS

Pared down by grief,
The light at the end of summer
Is more strange and ancient
Than all the remaindering stones
Of Rome.
Letting the days fall piecemeal
From the trees above us
Is like losing love
And letting the loss remain.

Birds of Mourning

There is this fact that only sorrow
Can undo the hung-up mind.
Fixated, thread-snagged,
It sometimes needs the fire,
The purifying dark:
Flame-lick, summer morbidity,
The decomposing dross of our lives
In ruin.
We circle round this sorrow
Like birds of mourning,
Eaters of sacrificial flesh.
In all these shade-ridden shrines
We do not find the cooling water
But another kind of thirst.
Something that makes the old maze blasé,
The old pains slough off
Like channels in the rain.
We are always orbiting our longing,
Discovering new circuits,
New gravities to chase.
We do not march forth
Straight into the truth
But hover in the same complexity
Of groves.
Learning, deepening: textures and angles,
The colors of the light.

WILD FISH

When you believe in something,
A green fish head rises through the night,
Breaks the sleeping waters
And takes a fatal gulp
From the upper air.

It's like this when you dream
We've all been here before,
That we have kissed and encircled
Each other with our arms
A thousand times and counting.

It's like this when you say
Some poor child came to turn
Our sufferings into grace,
To change our bodies
With his blood.

Each of these makes such strange
Aquatic gems
Come up for breath and tending,
An inverse sea of wonder
Slowly starting to flood

The decaying Roman gates.

OLD FRUIT

The empty socket where the world
Meets the eye
Is blown by sudden force
Against the ceiling's ledger.
This is how I'll go
When my bones can't stand the longing,
When the medication dances
Its final artificial spin
And love's crooked, unappeasable smile
Leaves me with the ghost it is.
It will be a Monday, I imagine,
And I'll be somewhere near the shore.
The dawn will be a field of birdsong
And the soul, that ancient mummified fruit,
Will fall back towards its heavenly vendors,
Eerie and oracular, on the whitened sea.

AUTUMN EQUATION

That luminous trail cannot be traced
By any hand.
It shuttles between worlds
Carrying the birds and their small apples.
One day, turning a corner, we may find
The wind has many sides.

December Rain

The rain will enter the branches
Of his hearing crossed as sable.
It's the only way that counts,
Blowing through his bones
Like torrential music,
Like inexactitude or loss.
Outside his window
The black-eyed Susans
Sustain and replicate the light.
They are bigger than his most
Astounding wealth,
Than any feat his singular mind
Can abate or conjure.
The beauty is that after the rain,
In the sudden slickness,
It all goes on like nothing.
The Bedouin clouds
Just keep on drifting,
Just keep passing overhead.
When he holds to his chest
His shaking, rain-soaked fingers,
The entire zodiac can be heard
With its dozen, star-shaped gears.

ALL AROUND US

It's the kind of snow that only falls once a century.
A miracle coming down in summer or the latter days of spring,
Bringing with it a cause for disbelief,
A reason to doubt the procedural seasons,
What we've been told of stasis and growth.
It's a thing that sometimes find us in a dream;
The hand turned towards what is usual,
The heart perched for the expected,
Then suddenly the confetti of some unreal light
Pouring in through the window
Like a gigantic matchstick
Filleting the dark.
It is not that for which we have waited,
The secret heartache of every lovely night,
But something else entirely:
A movement of music starting up from nowhere.
A piece of our old selves coming back.
Some blue otherness
Racing towards our lives.

DAYBREAK

On a day without obligations,
Covered by the first snowfall,
The whole country stares out
Of luminous windows, taking in
The altered landscape, the mares
Sleeping under white trees.
At the edge of his visions,
The oneironaut comes back
To this: a world of quieting forms.
He missed the entire summer
Peering into himself.
All those deep roads exit here.

WINTER MUSIC

This close to winter
Even the barest modes
Of listening
Cannot receive
The welded decibels
Transmitted by the stars.

Skull

Beside the flanks of white houses
The plants sing liquefying songs.
Their metallic voices are like
Drops of heavy paint,
Colorful molts from a dragon's side.
When I hear them,
I believe there is a festival
In the inner life of all things,
In the marrow, the deep materials.
A knot of music
That cracks open
Like a frozen skull.

NEGATIVE WEIGHT

Zodiacal light in the landscape of the deceased.
Banana slugs carrying wind-bruised bodies
To their kingdom beneath the leaves.
Above us, the moon as gorged
As someone's pet hyena.
In this place the stars are a
Reversed solution for seeing clear.
In ultimate blackness we say *Star-dark,*
The world clothed in snuffed-out lanterns.
Like bees painted in heavy coats of waxen ochre,
There is no shining in the flowers.
The field just beautifully dark
Between spliffs of color.
The soul, not twenty-one grams
Of calculable dust
But a negative weight
Tricking the scales.

SIDES

We must believe
The green leaves
Will reach us,
That the alabaster jars
Fill with second light,
That our faces turn
As a resting heron
Sometimes turns
Inwards, to a shining wing.

MONKS

The mushrooms lead nowhere
But into themselves,
Black stairways that end
In beautiful crevices
Between damp rocks
And delicate hands.
When you hold them,
Their whole drooping story
Fills the air.
You can almost taste them
Musting through your lungs.
It's the language of deep existence,
Of being rooted to something so big
You don't believe in edges.
It's why they are the holy men
Of the forest,
Always humble,
Hooded in prayer.

Evening in a Bottle

Excellent at subtraction,
The blue finch disappears
Into the blue expansion.
The fruit-shaped clouds
Take in the multicolored light,
And what remains is a blur
Of deeper colors,
A montage of hidden shades.
At this precise point
The water engulfs the
Swarms of fish;
The ocean becomes opaque,
Dark metal full of painted waves,
A smoky glass of specters.
Somewhere through the levels
Of depths and fractals,
The moon orbits into view,
Its pale face crosshatched
By scars of whitened sand.

Constellations

If there is something wrong
With this world,
I am blissfully unaware.
Deadpan, the hummingbird
Stares into the molecules of dew
And sees the color refracted.
It carries those rainbow particles
All day in its triple rhythm.
It's so fast, you'd never know
This is how the deposited sun
Turns into honey, into the sweetness
Of light.
Somewhere above us
The stars let down their radial tresses,
Tracing in the dark
The shape of a young boy
With his two cerulean jars.

Nectar

The prayer is dreaming all day
It is a butterfly coasting
The black stone and entering
The sky.
It leaves the mouth
To hinge on silence
And wait for the first
Rain of music.
How softly it hovers,
Like something almost said,
Like a hesitation, a longing
Never embodied.
Even among the flourish
Of carnations it is barely
A light, barely a shine
Or color.
The prayer opposes everything
We stand for by simply being prayer.
It is like the stream of invisible nectar
From which the gathering bees
Craft their wild gold.

The Garden

He comes into the garden
Because it is the only door
In the pervading mist.
It might be the back
Of the world, or only *the world*
Opening out from our illusions.
Snow falls like delicate white fruit,
Like fossilized sunlight.
He leans over the well
Where he can see constellations
Drifting above him.
He's been trying his whole life
To get here,
To taste that shimmering black water.
When he reaches down
Into that darkness,
The petals of a sunken ash tree
Fill his hands.

The Heart is an Odd-Shaped Shore

Banana palms and the light
Like old bedrock stripping the dark.
In this place where the river
Takes your name,
Where the soul chirps and buoys,
The ferryman is treading his way.
He is building a pattern
For our hearts to follow,
For the one in us who knows
The cardinal ricochet,
The leewarding drift
Towards home.
In the missing quadrants,
In the map's unmarked edges,
A bird is rising
Like a song-filled fist,
A ship full of secret wagers.
If we can unspool our glittering nets
And catch a single reddened streak
In the darkened waters,
Then even the iron-girdled weight
Of all our longing
Will suddenly burst
Like wild fruit.

Morning

I wake up in my own body,
And my blood and the green leaves
Form a cradle.
It must be a Sunday,
Because the boroughs are asleep
And someone is tending the alms.
A white rain is falling,
And the tracks of animals
Lead nowhere.
Their beautiful mirages
Walk us in a circle
Until we're standing
Where we started.
This *is* the exact center.
Nothing needs to change.
The light in our pupils
Reaches out, like a great
Wing taking in its young.

Modern Hearts

It was summer, maybe, because the moon
Was a warm thumbprint on cathedral glass,
And the fireflies sang hymns
As their tiny flames sailed up
Towards Cassiopeia, or some other darkness
Too distant to name,
And I lay down on the cool grass
To flip through my album of longings.
In Maine there is still more forest
Than most modern hearts can bear,
And it instilled in me a lifelong love
For secret places, for dark ravines
Where the snow makes small rivers.
Sometimes when I'm out of sync
With whatever metronome balances
Our lives, I think back to those
September forests, many of them now gone,
And I hold on fast to their variegated colors,
Their shimmering mirage of light.

THE HAUNTED

In the transept of the trees:
Bare, winter stones.
Then a voice, flush as a cellist
On fire.
Maybe a bird, maybe the brain's clicking
At the mind's unraveling.
Either way, a haunting. A mysterious presence
Rocking the heart's rafters,
The calcified planks far from sea.
In all this I can remember
But snatches of rain and waiting.
Drizzling afternoons when the music
Filled the corridors like spring
Or cooking;
When the ghost that is, or was, or will be,
Sang in the paintings on the wall.
Our startled eyes occasionally catching
His mercurial light
In one of Monet's blushes of blue.

Passages

He died in his sleep
And between the glints of nothing
A familiar blue world skirted by.
He became a mandala of lake stones,
A centripetal hole in the water's
Presence. The birds flew down
And peered into the center.
It shined like pupils,
Like sun on a winter surface.
When he awoke, everything was different.
The stars burned new patterns
In the amniotic night.

Anchors

Distillate faces
Going through
The eerie margins
To the place
Of crystallized light,
Of spacious winds
That blow all day
And never stop,
Never fade into
A grove of aspens.
We become ghosts,
Or maybe we become
Solid beings,
Always drifting back
To our lack of substance,
The mirage of colors
We call the soul.
In the port of final anchors
We set down
Our quiet golden weights,
The ones we have been
Building for many lives.
Eventually even the spectral
Captain fades.
We become those darkened stones.

GREEN THAUMATURGE

In the forest, a divulged tire
Has filled with fuchsia-colored snakes.

They appear radioactive, or maybe fed
With the blood of Redondo evenings.

Nearby, a hunter traps a hare
In a small cage. He's perplexed

To find it's made of glass, or maybe ice
Sculpted from the remaindered slags of Pangea.

When you hear a rustle,
You start looking for the flash

Of birds hoboing from limb
To limb.

What you find instead is a
Rapture-colored eye peering

At you through the leaves.
Over the landscape, clouds of white butterflies

Descend like omens.
You practice transfiguring

Their bodies into snow,
Accidentally creating winter

In the fire-petaled air.

THE PLACES WE LEAVE BEHIND

Those stars are slick as wet medallions,
Glass over Rangeley where the trees
Still whistle,
Where the wind's magnanimous
As an open palm.
Somewhere there is an unfractured meadow,
A matrix of timothy and milkweed,
Of white, abaxial leaves.
When the moon comes over
With its alien light,
It wraps around the house
In pythonic clarity.
Between its eyes
A single, beautiful stone
Erases everything.
Only the winter field remains.

STONES

In the thicket of night-blooming jasmine
A man who is an emissary of the moon
Gathers up golden pieces.
They are the remains of an old god,
Maybe goddess, shattered overhead
On a night dark as cinder rock,
A night so long ago
The inhabitants of myth
Call it myth.
Back in the world, no one believes
In the glittering stones.
They proclaim their silver veins
Full of fraudulence,
Throw them into the street
And slam the door behind him.
He carries the pieces with him
All his life, dropping them
Here and there on his journey
Across the continents.
Each one roots into the soil
Like a dimmed-down lantern.
When he dies they suddenly blossom,
Overturning the earth with their
Massive, shining trees.

BECOMING SERAPHIM

The ghost laments in the burnt-out foxglove,
Eats the ash-filled apples, the phantom fruits,
The blueness of death filling the air
Like early spring.

His body fades, and he feels the wind
Expand his organs.
They burst like bulbs at high voltage,
Like blood clots to the brain.

In their place, the simplicities of light,
Of hidden fractals,
Vanished joints that form new systems
Of bone,

Astral marrow, cartilage the color
Of forget-me-nots,
Nerves like new philosophies—
Hesitant at first, then ending civilizations.

Among the conifers, the brackish undergrowth,
The memory of stilted fields,
The ghost is growing hexagonal wings
Bright as camphor,

Is setting dark, unnerving eyes
Like hot stones in his panicked sockets.

UNEXPECTED GUESTS

Birds were lighting down
On the field,
Which held itself open
Like someone's ritual heart
Blossoming green.
We had never known ourselves
To be so happy with unexpected guests,
But our house had no walls
And the wind had already overturned
Everything at the table.
The wine could play no tricks
On such lucid company,
And I was no longer afraid
To let the narrative of my defeats
Fall to pieces.
I was simply happy to be alive.

The Sea Itself

No one comes to talk to you today.
The ships blown in from the sea,
The purple tigers defanged by water,
And everything we know of desire
Skinned like a cool fish.
From the hook of blossoms
Above the door,
A voice resembling the crooked
God of merchants
Asks for remuneration.
You almost die casting
It from your house.
It takes blood and poetry
And the last preserving grain
Of glowing salt.
Somewhere in all of this
A woman made of coral
Slipped in. It may have been
Through the window
On the seaweed-scented wind,
Or maybe through the staccatoed cracks.
Her voice is two-thirds surface light
And one-third subaqueous sun.
If you listen, she might lead you
To her kingdom of rust and stone,
To the ocean's glassblown heart,
To the lord of shipwrecks
Who, inversely, is also the lord
Of floating things.

THE WHALES

I don't remember exactly, but I dreamed
Of a wharf where something greater
Than ourselves washed in from the sea.
Everything we touch refers back to us.
We don't believe in anything.
But that sea was so immense, and our silhouettes
So small, that it seemed an undeniable rebuke.
I want only to know the shape of great things
Coming in from the horizon.
I want only to be told I barely matter.

Sea Glass

Sometimes the moon of this world
Comes down to incite your dreams.
It's a fire that knows no limits,
Enlarging in your head like a rage
Or vision,
Like a small silver thimble
Spilling oceans, magnitudes of light.
It burns off the day as one or two
Dropping tree limbs, shattering misconceptions,
Leaving you a stranger to yourself,
Cradled in sleep.
Sometimes the moon of this world
Is a totem we carry with us,
An assurance that when the time is right
There will be a passage, a conduit home.
Sometimes it is simply a flame
Going wild in your heart, in the sky,
In your hands where it becomes
A million shining vigils,
A trove of weathered glass.

ABSENCE

Upon waking
Only the birds
Are familiar,
A fitful yellow
Between the trees.
Am I one of them
Or something else completely?
In the absence
Of a narrative
My life falls
To pieces.
They are clouds
Blown in from nowhere.
Far from the need
To be afraid, what I glimpse
Is emptiness shining.
Even in the disparaging loss
I can feel
That rigorous light
Behind my eyes.

Happiness

Grief sings on an axis
Dead center in the heart,
In the one delicate place
Where trees won't grow,
Where love is intimated
But never found.
It is an absence
But charges the air
With soot,
With unmovable disbelief,
A wrongheaded faith
In nothing.
The only way to escape
Is to observe how the
Surrounding forest rustles,
How the branches are unburdened.
You must deduce
The presence of the crane,
Freshly lifted out of darkness
And on its way to somewhere new.

Last Sleep

Suddenly I am no one.
Evening fills its brass jars
With ichorous grass,
And the sadness that made
The moon a cold stone
Instead of an angel
Floats down to ruin
Even this one good night.
It's not that the logician
Doesn't hold the key
To certain things,
But I remember, when I
Came upon bent stalks
In the forest, they shined
With the unicorn's last sleep
And I travelled on, looking
For its radiant trail.
You convinced me it wasn't there,
Was never there; and I still walk
Around carrying that irreparable darkness,
That hole in my reason where
The continuum of ancient things
Once held us closely
To the rabbit-colored earth.

Turnabout

You park the car in a place
Where the headlights are
Overwhelmed by darkness,
Where the radio fades
Into the migrant static,
The negating air.
Mars moves into the rearview mirror
Like some creature of the night
With its one red eye.
You don't believe in war,
But your blood recognizes
The call and pounds inside you.
All around, the lilacs fill your breathing,
Barely perceptible, in-breath and out.
You don't have to be anything
For anyone, not even the gods.
The field breaks open like a heart.

PENUEL

Although there are no absolutes,
A blue wing once settled
In a green valley and it was
Unmistakably beautiful.
I don't know what it was
Because it was gone
Before the taxonomist could name it.
Bird or insect? Perhaps a mirage
Of rushing light?
It set down like snow,
And for a moment the middle air
Was wondrously alive
With grace and altercation.

ACKNOWLEDGMENTS

The author wishes to gratefully acknowledge the journals in which many of these poems first appeared:

Abyss & Apex: "Populating the Dark"
Allegro Poetry Magazine: "Remainders"
Anima: "An Exchange of Wonder"
Black Fox Literary Magazine: "Absence"
Calamus Journal: "Broken Hulls," "Into Matter"
Change Seven: "Old Fruit"
The Charles Carter: "Evening in a Bottle"
Chiron Review: "Two Worlds"
Clear Poetry: "Sea Glass"
Corvus Review: "The Glassmaker"
The Courtship of Winds: "Autumn Equation," "Horse Valley
    Nocturne," "Seasoning the Ship of Death"
Fredericksburg Literary and Art Review: "The Heart is an
    Odd-Shaped Shore"
Gingerbread House: "The Alchemist"
Gravel: "All This Singing"
The Halcyon Reader: "Negative Weight"
Hartskill Review: "Wild Fish"
HeartWood: "Monks"
Hermes Poetry Journal: "Moonstruck"
The Ibis Head Review: "Modern Hearts"
Kaleidotrope: "The Sea Itself"
Lady Lazarus Journal: "Conduit"
The Literary Nest: "Birds of Mourning"
The Magnolia Review: "Explorers"
Mithila Review: "Green Thaumaturge,' "Stones"
MockingHeart Review: "Ghost"
Modern Poetry Quarterly Review: "Becoming Seraphim"
Muddy River Poetry Review: "Sides"
Mystic Blue Review: "Calando," "Night Fable," "Passages,"
    "The Sleepwalker"
Occulum: "Skull"

Pretty Owl Poetry: "Declension Music"
River River: "All Around Us"
Rose Red Review: "Anchors"
Sheila-Na-Gig Online: "Constellations," "Nectar," "The Garden"
Sliver of Stone: "Turnabout"
Subprimal Poetry Art: "In the Rotary Silence of Seasons"
Thirteen Ways Magazine: "Being Here"
TreeHouse-An Exhibition of the Arts: "Last Sleep"
Two Cities Review (Featured Writers Blog): "Waking Up"
VAYAVYA: "Horses"
Visitant: "Night Birds"
Yellow Chair Review: "What's Gathered There"
Zetetic—A Record of Unusual Inquiry: "Botany"

About FutureCycle Press

FutureCycle Press is dedicated to publishing lasting English-language poetry books, chapbooks, and anthologies in both print-on-demand and Kindle ebook formats. Founded in 2007 by long-time independent editor/publishers and partners Diane Kistner and Robert S. King, the press incorporated as a nonprofit in 2012. A number of our editors are distinguished poets and writers in their own right, and we have been actively involved in the small press movement going back to the early seventies.

The FutureCycle Poetry Book Prize and honorarium is awarded annually for the best full-length volume of poetry we publish in a calendar year. Introduced in 2013, our Good Works projects are anthologies devoted to issues of universal significance, with all proceeds donated to a related worthy cause. Our Selected Poems series highlights contemporary poets with a substantial body of work to their credit; with this series we strive to resurrect work that has had limited distribution and is now out of print.

We are dedicated to giving all of the authors we publish the care their work deserves, making our catalog of titles the most diverse and distinguished it can be, and paying forward any earnings to fund more great books.

We've learned a few things about independent publishing over the years. We've also evolved a unique, resilient publishing model that allows us to focus mainly on vetting and preserving for posterity poetry collections of exceptional quality without becoming overwhelmed with bookkeeping and mailing, fundraising activities, or taxing editorial and production "bubbles." To find out more about what we are doing, come see us at www.futurecycle.org.

The FutureCycle Poetry Book Prize

All full-length volumes of poetry published by FutureCycle Press in a given calendar year are considered for the annual FutureCycle Poetry Book Prize. This allows us to consider each submission on its own merits, outside of the context of a contest. Too, the judges see the finished book, which will have benefitted from the beautiful book design and strong editorial gloss we are famous for.

The book ranked the best in judging is announced as the prize-winner in the subsequent year. There is no fixed monetary award; instead, the winning poet receives an honorarium of 20% of the total net royalties from all poetry books and chapbooks the press sold online in the year the winning book was published. The winner is also accorded the honor of being on the panel of judges for the next year's competition; all judges receive copies of all contending books to keep for their personal library.

88997415R00048

Made in the USA
Lexington, KY
21 May 2018